What tools do we use...?

At school

Vic Parker

Heinemann
LIBRARY

Little Nippers

H **www.heinemann.co.uk/library**
Visit our website to find out more information about **Heinemann Library** books.

To order:
☎ Phone 44 (0) 1865 888066
🖹 Send a fax to 44 (0) 1865 314091
💻 Visit the Heinemann Bookshop at www.heinemann.co.uk/library to browse our
catalogue and order online.

First published in Great Britain by Heinemann
Library, Halley Court, Jordan Hill, Oxford
OX2 8EJ, part of Harcourt Education.
Heinemann is a registered trademark of Harcourt
Education Ltd.

Editorial: Jilly Attwood and Louise Galpine
Design: Jo Hinton-Malivoire and bigtop,
Bicester, UK
Models made by: Jo Brooker
Picture Research: Rosie Garai
Production: Séverine Ribierre

Originated by Dot Gradations
Printed and bound in China by South China
Printing Company

ISBN 0 431 17151 3 (hardback)
07 06 05 04 03
10 9 8 7 6 5 4 3 2 1

ISBN 0 431 17156 4   (paperback)
07 06 05 04 03
10 9 8 7 6 5 4 3 2 1

British Library Cataloguing in Publication Data
Parker, Vic
What tools do we use ...? At school
371.6'7
A full catalogue record for this book is available
from the British Library.

Acknowledgements
The publishers would like to thank the following
for permission to reproduce phototgraphs:
Gareth Boden pp.**4**, **5**, **6**, **7**, **8/9**, **10/11**, **12**, **13**,
14, **15**, **16**, **17**, **19**, **20**, **21**; Gareth Boden and
Getty Images pp.**22/23**; Getty Images p.**18**.

Cover photograph reproduced with permission of
Gareth Boden.

The publishers would like to thank Annie Davy
for her assistance in the preparation of this book.

Every effort has been made to contact copyright
holders of any material reproduced in this book.
Any omissions will be rectified in subsequent
printings if notice is given to the publishers.

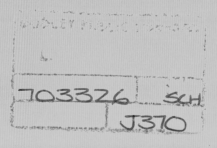

Contents

Tools at school

When teacher writes, she uses a blackboard, chalk and board rubber.

Writing tools

What do you use to write with?

Do you keep your pencil sharp with a pencil sharpener?

Drawing tools

How many colours do you know?

Painting tools

A paintbrush is perfect for painting a picture, but hands can be just as handy!

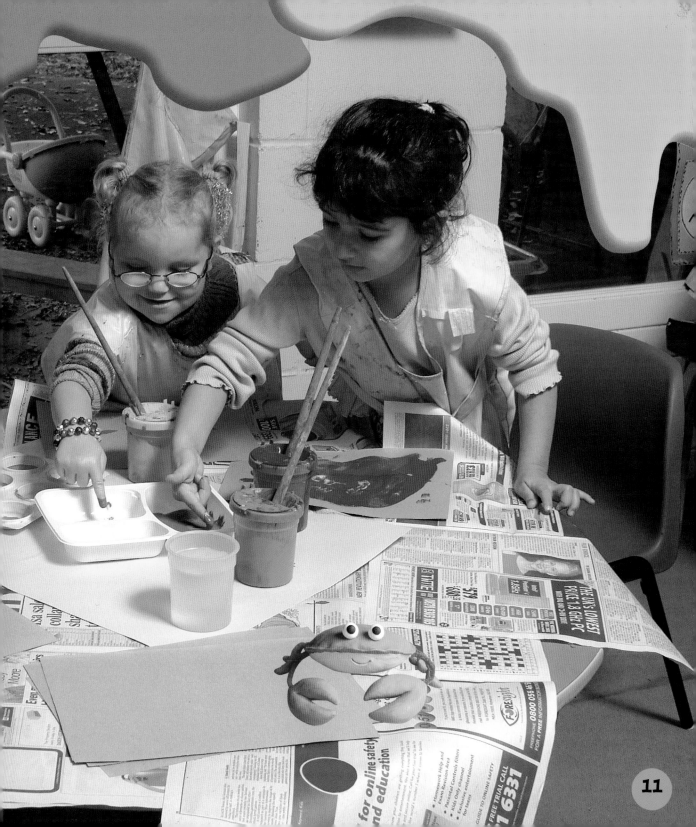

Tools for making things

What would you make?

Glue

13

Counting tools

One

Two

Three

Four

Use the blocks to count some more.

An abacus helps to make sums simple.

Tools for joining things

Can you guess what all these tools do?

They join pieces of paper together!

Finding out tools

A magnifying glass makes small

things look HUGE

so you can see them better.

Books and computers can help you find out about things too.

Telling the time tools

When is it time to go back indoors?

21

What are these school tools?

scissors

paint brush

pencil

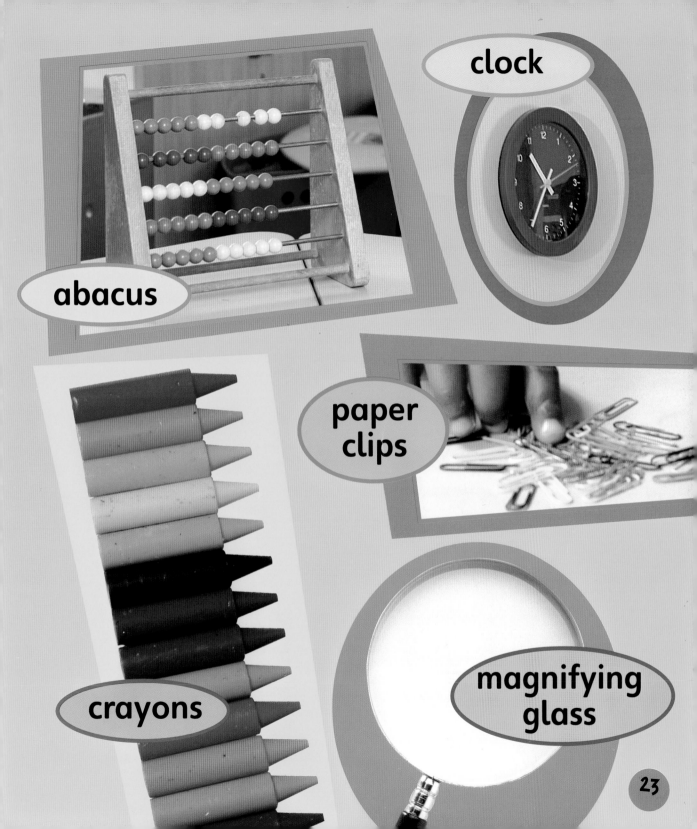

clock

abacus

paper clips

crayons

magnifying glass

23

Index

The end

Notes for adults

'What tools do we use . . .?' explores a variety of tools that a young child may come across in different situations. The series encourages young children to think creatively about the different jobs these tools do, and what other tools they might use to do the same job. The books provide opportunities for discussing how the tools should be used safely and correctly, and what materials the tools are made from. There are four titles in the series: *At school*, *At home*, *In the kitchen*, and *In the garden*. Used together, the books will enable comparison of similarities and differences between a wide variety of tools.

The key curriculum Early Learning Goals relevant to this series are:
• learn skills by using a range of tools
• select tools and techniques necessary to shape, assemble and join a range of materials
• talk about tools and their effects and how they work
• realize that tools can be used for a purpose and introduce children to appropriate tools to work on different materials
• encourage children to use the correct names for tools.

This book introduces the reader to a range of tools they may use at school. The book will help children extend their vocabulary, as they will hear new words such as *abacus* and *magnifying glass*. You may like to introduce and explain other new words yourself, such as *hole punch*, *paper clips* and *stapler*.

Additional information about tools
A tool is defined as any object which you use to perform an operation to achieve an end. Tools can be small, like pencils, or large, like lawn mowers. Tools can be hand-held, such as screwdrivers, or stationary, such as pasta-making machines. Tools can be manual, like saws, or power-driven, such as hair-dryers. Tools can be classified by their function, such as: joining things or shaping things; by their mode of operation, such as: sticking things or cleaning things; or by their mode of action, such as: tools that cut, tools that mix, tools that suck.

Follow-up activities
• Make a picture using lots of different writing and drawing tools: chalks, pencils, crayons, markers, paints etc.
• Make a model using tools that stick and join things: glue, sticky tape, a stapler, a hole punch etc.

24